LET THE MOON WOBBLE

LET THE MOON WOBBLE

ALLY ANG

Alice James Books

NEW GLOUCESTER, MAINE

alicejamesbooks.org

10 9 8 7 6 5 4 3 2 1

Alice James Books are published by Alice James Poetry Cooperative, Inc.

Alice James Books
Auburn Hall
60 Pineland Drive, Suite 206
New Gloucester, ME 04260
www.alicejamesbooks.org

Library of Congress Cataloging-in-Publication Data

Names: Ang, Ally author
Title: Let the moon wobble : poems / Ally Ang.
Description: New Gloucester, Maine : Alice James Books, 2025.
Identifiers: LCCN 2025020184 (print) | LCCN 2025020185 (ebook) | ISBN
    9781949944884 trade paperback | ISBN 9781949944501 epub
Subjects: LCGFT: Poetry
Classification: LCC PS3601.N5529977 L48 2025 (print) | LCC PS3601.N5529977
    (ebook) | DDC 811/.6--dc23/eng/20250530
LC record available at https://lccn.loc.gov/2025020184
LC ebook record available at https://lccn.loc.gov/2025020185

Alice James Books gratefully acknowledges support from individual donors, private
foundations, the National Endowment for the Arts, and the Poetry Foundation
(https://www.poetryfoundation.org).

Cover art: "Swimmers Outer Space" cover painting by Katherine Bradford

CONTENTS

PART THREE

Holes of the world, open up your lids and howl!

—**KIM HYESOON,** *All the Garbage of the World, Unite!*
Translated by Don Mee Choi

INVOCATION

Let the moon wobble.

Let the basil plant flower.

Let the poets discombobulate.

Let the verbs noun. Let the nouns verb.

Let the grief howl.

Let the emails unread.

Let the land speak.

Let the oceans revenge.

Let the people free. Let

the people free.

LET THE MOON WOBBLE, PART ONE

QUARS POETICA

Because I'm as lonely
        as a swan is mean, so lonely
that I would kiss the putrid feet

of anyone who glanced my way.
        Because last night I dreamed I ran
into a friend in the aisles

of a used bookstore, touched
        his arm as though neither of us
could die. Because as a child, I hid

my smile in photographs so that my eyes
        wouldn't crinkle into slits, trained
the muscles of my face to stay taut

and demure, wide-eyed, never revealing
        too much. Now, I wear my gibbous-moon grin
like a rhinestone necklace, gaudy

and astonishing, unafraid of my crinkle-eyed
        joy. Because the dead burrow
into the spaces between each word I write. Each line

broken and unbroken. So I wrap myself
        in a weighted blanket meant to imitate
human touch, bask in the SAD lamp's

synthetic light, write another poem.
        Delete. Begin again.

KUBURAN CINA BINTARO

Two years after my grandfather's death, we gather in the cemetery
        to burn. Not even five feet tall,

my grandfather made his living as a traveling bra salesman
        until the genocide. On the day of his death,

I snotted and sobbed my way through my college a cappella concert
        even though he was, in effect, a stranger

whom I probably never loved. At the cemetery in Ampenan,
        we lay offerings on his grave, fresh oranges and sweet cakes,

to invite him to feast. Soon, he will arrive to fill his big ghost belly
        while my family laughs and chatters in a language I don't understand.

Inside a perfect miniature house, they have placed
        televisions, cars, stacks of money, even tiny paper servants,

to set aflame and send up to him in the afterlife
        so that he will live (or, rather, not live) like a king.

Does this mean that ghosts have capitalism too? I whisper to my partner
        who shrugs, unbothered. *What do you think?* I ask my grandfather

while we wait for midnight. He doesn't answer, but I know that he is here
        by the way that the trees refuse to crack a smile.

The first flames lap up the foundation like a dog in the hot sun,
        shadows twisting faces into unfamiliar masks.

The house crumbles into ash like a body
        crumbles into ash. *What will be left, kakek,*

after everything has burned?

SPRING IN SEATTLE

How many synonyms
are there for *gray*, or
endless, or *as mushy*
as an overcooked casserole?
I take the mountains
for granted, let my calls
go to voicemail, my heart
hollowing like canned
sitcom laughter. Outside
my window, a woman
and her dachshund parade
down the street wearing
matching Burberry sweaters
while the rents skyrocket
into the stratosphere.
I practice patience, water
my similes, wait for them
to overtake the front lawn.
Hummingbirds hover like
tiny surveillance drones.
Every day is a minute
longer than the one before.
I cradle each minute of light
in my hands like a pearl.

ANTI-ODE TO GIRLHOOD

Before I was a girl, I was an accusation. A bad
omen. A piece of gum stuck to the bottom
of my mother's boot. As hard as her body tried
to scrape me off, I would not budge. Like any good
daughter, I learned the art of swallowing
my humiliation. Lowered my eyes in reverence
of older girls, eavesdropped on their bathroom
whisperings, drunk off the secondhand thrill
of their first tentative touches. Kept my hair long
and my fingernails trimmed. Waited patiently

for God to reach their divine hand between my legs
and make Something happen, but all that came
to me was a lack of breasts and a burgeoning must-
ache. I shape-shifted my way into denim skirts
and AOL chat rooms trying to reach
you, glittery blue shadow caked onto my eyelids
and bleach stinging my upper lip. In line
for the drugstore checkout, I snuck glances
at glossy magazine covers, memorizing headlines
like scripture, then tallying my shortcomings
in front of the mirror. How could I have known
then what singular, monstrous thing you would make
of me? Night after night, I placed
a tampon under my pillow in the hopes
that you would come to me, that someday,
I too might bleed.

THE MOON, ABSTRACTED

by clouds, becomes a symbol
for longing. From a safe distance,

a poet will romanticize anything:
pale lifeless rock, hurtling through

oblivion, greedily siphoning
light. The cages, abstracted

by freedom, become a symbol
for inconvenience. *This is like prison,*

the woman across the aisle groans
when we're stuck for an extra half hour

on the tarmac. As though the cells,
the shackles, the people they suffocate

and surveil, are nothing more than
symbol or simile. The bombs, abstracted

by comfort. By the snow flurrying
out the window and the steam swirling

up from the teakettle on the stove.
The deaths, abstracted by syntax:

the children were killed. The women
were killed. The men were killed.

Subjects absent. Violence erased.
The deaths, abstracted by language.

The same language I use to make
poems, to fall in love, to chant

in the streets and share in the ritual
of grief. The same language that

murders, incarcerates, declares
bodies illegal when they refuse

submission. I want to say what really
matters, and I want to say it plain.

May every colonial regime collapse
within our lifetime. May each border

crumble into dust. From Palestine
to West Papua, from Puerto Rico

to Hawai'i, from Congo to Sudan,
from the river to the sea. May every

martyr's memory take root in the soil
of a liberated land. May every

oppressed tongue know the taste
of water, honey, freedom, freedom.

SELF-PORTRAIT WITH CROPPED HAIR

I paint self-portraits because I am so often alone, because I am the person I know best.
—FRIDA KHALO

This time, you must meet
my steadfast gaze. Watch
as I unmarry each strand

from my scalp, the scissors
a phantom limb in my grip,
metal as sharp as grief. Don't

turn away. As a child, I was told
that a woman's hair is her crowning
glory, but this keratin kingdom

lies limp and lifeless at the feet
of a vengeful god. *My beauty,*
you used to call me, taming

my hair with your fingers, held
in your eyes like an insect
pinned inside a frame. This is how

I demand to be seen: dressed
in my finest silk suit and shiniest
high heels, neither beautiful

nor yours. And when they say,
*What a pity, she was so pretty
once,* the dark strands on the ground

will writhe in reply.

RISK ASSESSMENT

Where did you come from?

> *I have spent / the currency of my body / clawing*
> *my way out / of the blood-dark dirt /*
> *that birthed me /*

Do you know why you are here?

> *O nation of filth / O great gaping maw / I pledge*
> *allegiance / to your oblivion /*
> *when I go waltzing into my grave / I will drag*
> *you down with me*

Is there a history of mental illness in your family?

> *call it what you must: illness / or empire /*
> *the prognosis is the same / those unforgiving*
> *hands / narrowing their orbit / around my neck*

Have you had thoughts of hurting yourself or others?

> *I knuckle the knots / out of my creaky back /*
> *harden my flesh to marble / and swallow*
> *the cracked shards of myself / that I have*
> *meticulously chiseled away*

Do you feel hopeless about the future?

> *does the android feel hopeless about its lack /*
> *of consciousness, or does it simply / fulfill*
> *its function?*

Have you ever attempted suicide?

> *when a starfish finds itself trapped / in a predator's*
> *grip / it will detach its captive limb / in order*
> *to escape / softening the connective tissue / until it drifts*
> *onto the ocean floor / like a rotting apple /*
> *some species can even regenerate / an entire body*
> *from a scrap / of severed arm / guided*
> *by stubborn instinct / a slow, bloodless miracle*

SEND NUDES

Though the world ended, desire
did not. In the absence of touch,
our imaginations spilled over
like watercolors. I read about an app
that could control, from a distance,
a lover's orgasm. I watched
through a screen as the technology
of sex adapted to touchlessness.
The camera became my beloved, a portal
through which I viewed myself sliced
into fragments, wracked with longing
to be seen in places a photograph
could not reach. My nerves deadened
from disuse; my hunger outgrew
the cage I built for it. I lay awake
while it rattled the bars and howled
until I could bear it no longer—I took
a jagged shard of my flesh and un-
leashed my desire. It folded me
into its arms, then consumed me.
Sucked the muscle and marrow
off my bones until they were white
and glistening. *Am I beautiful now?*
I asked my longing. The click
of the camera was the only
reply. Hit send.

WHAT DOESN'T KILL ME / MAKES ME

The man on the bus calls me
a █████, the effort of his hatred

peppering his brow with sweat,
and I wonder what gave me away.

I'm on my way to see my love,
cradling a grocery-store bouquet

in my arms. The stems begin
to wilt in my suffocating grip.

I don't want to tell you what
he said next, how he screamed

at me and the other █████s, the ways
he fantasized about our mutilation,

how the other men watched
and grinned like it was all a joke.

I don't want to admit I was afraid.
If my body were as dangerous

as a man's fear of it, I would
arm myself with my self and kill

the cop in my head. I would burn
down the cages. I would rob

enough banks to buy a cottage
to share with everyone I've ever

called home. Later, my love will hold
me while I cry silently, will refuse

to turn away from the snot and salt
leaking out of me. If I remove

the man from this poem, what will
be left? The flowers, exclamations

of yellow as sweet as late summer
sunshine. The way the other █████s

on the bus asked, *You okay?*
made unstrangers by circumstance,

finding ways to make each other
laugh. How my love sliced me

strawberries in the shape of hearts
while I unraveled in their bed,

their love the answer to a question
I didn't even know I had asked.

SOFT BOILED EGG

I have placed all my secrets in my sports bra
for safekeeping, where they stay sweet
and sticky like mochi. I feed them to you
in spoonfuls over the phone as we drift in
and out of silence. *I think the dahlias*
forgot to bloom this year, you say
as a way of saying nothing. How do I love
the things I cannot touch? I want to say it then,
but my guts are gently boiling, a soft yolk
of emotion cooking in my belly.
You say good night, and your voice rubs
against my clit like the seam of my jeans.
I reach for you, but you're already gone.
There's an itch in the crook
of my elbow where your head
used to rest.

UPDATES REGARDING [ ]

Dear [blistering moonlight slivered by blinds] [fruit fly circling an overripe banana] [succulent sickly with overwatering],

I hope this email finds you [stuffing your cavernous pit with the best garbage money can buy] [salting the earth with toothless anger] [snarling and snapping over scraps].

In these unprecedented times of [live-streamed obliteration] [window-smashed banks and blazing precincts] [bodies littering the Capitol steps], it is important to [pay your tithes] [confess your most salacious sins] [aim your ire into the pig's trough].

Now more than ever, we need you to [keep your hands and holes inside the vehicle] [disembowel your outrage] [avert your eyes when the bombs / when the guns / when the cops / when the smoke / when the illness / gets your neighbor] [just be glad it's not you].

Wishing you and your loved ones [a lie sweet enough to soothe] [a lung strong enough to withstand its labor] [an abundance of silkiest two-ply].

To unsubscribe to this email list, click [submit].

JUNE 23, 1982

for Vincent Chin

Vincent shyly kissing his fiancée at the bar
egged on by his friends' pillowing laughter

Vincent, face warm and aglow
after just two beers

Vincent, pulling a strand of her shiny black hair
off the sleeve of his coat and tucking it
into his breast pocket

Vincent, mother's only baby, assuring her
that this would be his last time going out
before his wedding day

Vincent, his mother clucking her tongue
in disapproval, reminding him that it's bad luck
to say *last time*

Vincent stumbling into the night
crooked teeth and bruised knuckles
taunting, *Is that all you've got?*

Vincent, stalked to the hunting ground
skin yellowing
beneath the artificial light
of the towering neon arches

Vincent: the baseball bat swinging
for a home run, his death
america's favorite pastime

Vincent, skull an overripe peach
spilling onto asphalt

18

Vincent, whose killers are *good boys,*
not the kind of men you send to jail

Vincent, wedded to dirt

Vincent, $3000 price tag
taped to his coffin

Vincent, some call it a deadly case
of mistaken identity, but

Vincent, in their eyes
we are all the same

MORE AMERICANS BELIEVE THEY'VE SEEN A GHOST THAN A TRANS PERSON

There, making love in the gender-neutral bathroom of a gay bar
atop a throne lined with toilet paper and grime, two ghosts.

Beads of sweat stippling galaxies onto their brown skin,
bodies heaving with aliveness like brand-new ghosts.

Their entanglement of limbs so beautiful, you shudder
with envy. You: a silent witness, the true ghost.

You've heard all the names for this—a spectacle, a dis-
grace, a revolution—but nothing comes close to *ghost*.

Is this memory or a mirror, the familiar voice calling your name
beneath the blanket of sleep, asking, *Who are you, ghost*?

LET THE MOON WOBBLE (PART TWO

I CALL GRIEF BY MY MOTHER'S NAME

[1]

[2]

[3]

[4]

[5]

[6]

---

[1] disobedient not-thing / refusing to die / some days / you believe that grief / has given birth to you / that there was no You / before It

[2] grief makes a vessel of you / like water / takes the shape of its container / seeping in / through the cracks / in the floorboards / through the membrane / of your cells / settling into the quiet / of this poem

[3] it finds you / small and abandoned / curled into a question mark / endlessly repeating / mouth wide / with unvoiced prayer:

[4] *O God / O God / O God*

[5] lie down / in the belly of this poem / until it swells / with your sadness / let your child heart / sink into sleep / at its breast

[6] dear Poet / you cannot silence your grief / forever / you can only welcome it / home.

I'M ASHAMED TO SAY IT OUT LOUD

But the scent of blood through denim
is a thick perfume of need, slickening
my other lips. I have no words
to ask for what I want: to coat you
with my filth, then lick it clean.
My belly is bloated with excess
ache, so hot it could melt
the silicone between us. Let me wet
your phantom limb and choke
on my apology. Each touch is a soft
error, a new stain on the comforter,
another bullet point in my list
of embarrassments, but my full mouth
can't stop begging even though I know
it's impolite. I'm sorry. My uterus
is too heavy to move. Let's just lie
here instead.

THE TRUTH IS

This is a multiple choice test.
Please answer to the best
of your ability.

1. Define *memory*:
   a) the hum of static prickling across a screen
   b) an insulated coffin
   c) an unwanted inheritance
   d) a trickster god

2. What have you lost?
   a) the careful choreography of beauty
      i)   arch your back
      ii) suck in your gut
      iii) lower your gaze
   b) an ardent devotion to my own
      destruction
      i)   lower your gaze
   c) another apology stuck in the brambles
      of my clumsy tongue

3. Which version of the story is closest
   to the truth?
   a) I was so lonely, I would have let anyone touch me
   b) I was shrouded in loneliness so thick
      that it was impossible to touch me
   c) I was born already fearful
                                    of touch

4. Yes, but what *really* happened?
   a) I gulped gallons of guilt   hoping it would fill
      the emptiness in me
   b) this alien vessel   this gift   this burden
      I've been told belongs to me

c) or did I ask   for my undoing?
d) I'm sorry
e)   I have made something
                    out of nothing
                again

   3. Which version of the story is
      the truth?
      a) I waited   like a dog   left tied
         to a chain-link fence   trembling
                  beneath the stark   starless sky
      b) too tired to sleep   I purged
         my mind of its memories   until I was

                 a stark starless sky
      c) despite my grasping, the truth
         slipped
                              through my fingers
                                    leaving me stark

      as a starless sky

5. Now that you've said all this, can you finally be happy?
   a) that's not
      the point

5. The truth is:
   a) I quench my bottomless thirst
      with saltwater   and spit
   b) I have imagined myself
        i)   as victim
        ii)   as martyr
        iii)   as   villain
        iv)   as   machine
   c) sometimes, a body is nothing more than a vehicle
      for memory

I set it to autopilot and wait

for its mal-

function

PAP SMEAR

The receptionist hands me a survey:
How many sexual partners have you had?
Are they male or female? I lie

like I always do. The magazine in the waiting room
tells me that I can get a flat stomach
from a diet of quinoa and asparagus. My stomach

is not flat. It hangs over the front of my jeans
like a coin purse bursting with organs. The doctor
asks if I have a boyfriend, if he treats me nice,

while she spreads my legs. One foot
into the stirrup, then the other. *You may experience*
some slight discomfort. A shock of cold metal

disrupts my breath, curls my toes
while the exam table paper crinkles
beneath bare flesh. I have opinions

about the instrument of violence
holding my body open, its history
too brutal for metaphor, but I keep them

to myself. The doctor makes me laugh while her hand
is inside me and it's just like love, except she is also
scraping cells from my cervical canal.

When she's done, she leaves the room while I re-dress
under the guise of modesty, as though
she was not just elbow-deep in the warmest

parts of me. I pray that my results will come back
clear, that my cells will not be found wanting.

I leave the office, microscopically smaller than I was before.

DENTISTRY

Clean as a Clorox-wiped countertop.
No cavities
in your sinless mouth. You prefer your grapes
free of seeds, your orange juice
without pulp. At the breakfast table
you pull one of my hairs out
from between your teeth, a keratin thread
of dental floss, and wish on it
before you let it fall. I want
to kiss you then, but you're already late
for work and I don't want to smudge
your lipstick. At night, I listen
to you brushing your teeth, bristles furious
against enamel. In my cup of chamomile
a single black hair clings to porcelain.
A tiny coiled phone cord. I fish it out
with the tip of my thumbnail.

ALL GIRLS GO TO HEAVEN

even the ones whose retainers   collect dust under the bed   the ones who kiss

with their eyes open   the ones who dog-ear   their library books

who forget   their mother's birthday   but still remember

their 3rd-grade crush's   home phone number   yes   all girls go to heaven

even the ones   who aren't girls   at all but something   far murkier

the lovesick   the fatherless   the ungovernable   and uncouth

I've heard that heaven   looks just like this: everyone you love

in side-by-side sleeping bags   stoned off acetone   and hushed secrets

holding your best friend's hand   until you fall asleep   the summer

stretching endlessly ahead of you   as invincible and full   as the moon.

NOBODY OWNS MY PLEASURE

Through a sliver of doorframe it slinks
into my body, a full-bellied cat

knocking over the knickknacks in its path,
demanding my attention even as I deny it.

Fingernails carve down
the small of my back, metal thuds

against meat. My lover's arms encircle me.
In the eye, I unspool.

The rope digs into my flesh as I spill
out of my skin, onto the carpet, a senseless

shuddering mess. I used to want to be
beautiful, which is another way of wanting

to be seen. Now I fear the years
I spent hating my body may out

-number the years I have left to inhabit it.
At most angles I am a stranger

to myself, wary of the light that blushes
my hips. If you'd told me it was possible

to be touched like this I wouldn't
have believed you. A hand aching

at my throat, my blood shining, wet, no
-body owns my pleasure. Not even me.

AUTOEROTIC ABECEDARIAN

At the apex of night, limbs splayed across the too-small
bed, I allow my hands to wander towards the heat of my
cunt, desire sharp and pulsing. Beneath the shawl of
darkness, I shape my flesh like a block of clay, all its
excess overflowing onto the sheets. The smooth
flat landscape of my chest ballooning with breath, teeth
grinding like derelict machinery. In the slick heat of
here, I become my self: an embodiment of purest
instinct. The scent of my want intoxicating enough to
justify its undoing. Before I even knew my body, I
knew its catalog of disgrace: the insatiable blood-
lust, the propensity for leakage. Shame,
my familiar shadow, undress me with your
needy mouth, your gnarled fingers. I am
open and waiting for you to make a
private spectacle of me. Do you hear it, the
quickening of my heart? The volatile
rhythm of unrepentant rapture, my insides
spilling onto the carpet like a pool of mercury.
Tired of all these selfish lovers, I
undulate my hips under my
voracious hand, wet and shining
with want, unfurling like a
xeranthemum inside me. Shame,
you unwelcome god, at the
zenith of my pleasure, you are there.

POSTOPERATIVE CARE

My mother dozes open-mouthed in a hospital bed
while I grind my teeth at her bedside.
Contorted in pain even as she sleeps,
her face is a mirror of my own.

I grind my teeth at her bedside,
swallowing my desire to turn away
from her face, a mirror of my own:
thin-skinned, sun-touched, love-swollen.

I swallow my desire to turn away
when I see my reflection in the hospital bed.
Thin-skinned, sun-touched, love-swollen—
she is small in the sea of blankets.

When I see my reflection in the hospital bed,
I remember where I came from.
Once, I was small in a sea of blankets
while she cradled me through sleepless nights.

I can never forget where I come from:
a love capable of reimagining the world.
Once, she held me close on sleepless nights.
Now, I hold her hand as she sleeps

open-mouthed in a hospital bed.

AFTER PROLONGED GRIEF DISORDER WAS ADDED TO THE DSM-5

Grief in these circumstances is normal, but not at certain levels
and not most of the day, nearly every day, for months.
—VIVIAN B. PENDER, American Psychiatric Association President

Today, my heart is working
remotely. I watch it thump
and thrum reliably behind
the blur of a computer screen.
A man with a gun opens fire
in a subway car. I refresh
my emails and reheat the stale
remnants of my morning
coffee. A dull twinge of dread
crystallizes in my throat. When
I type *Asian woman* into Google,
the algorithm helpfully suggests:
killed / attacked / stabbed /
shoved onto the train tracks /
hit by a baseball bat. I hit
refresh again. A war breaks
out far enough away to be
a safe abstraction. *Thank god*
we can finally get back to
normal, an acquaintance sighs,
as though the millions dead
can be swatted out of sight
like a mosquito on a humid
summer night, smushed against
a paper towel, one stubborn
limb still twitching until
it stops. The employee
handbook reads, *Don't forget*
to clock out before you let
the fragile ceiling of your sanity

shatter around you! Don't
forget to sweep up the shards
on your way out! I confess:
I am bored of my heartbreak.
I am tired of writing this poem,
this elegy, trying to find some
assemblage of language to make
sense of the senseless, flailing
my futile limbs against the cruel
engine of capital as it grinds
relentlessly toward
a singular, griefless end.

HEARTBREAK MAD LIBS

There are _____ ways of looking at _____ .
# of your lover's hairs stuck   _most recent catastrophe_
in the shower drain

Today, _____ is brighter than it's ever been. The sky is _____ and
     celestial body   _color of the birthmark_
thick with _____ .   _on your left inner thigh_
       words you wish you'd
       said before they left

_____ people have _____ for you to be here today. Can you
# of times you've forgotten to call   _action verb ending in -ed_
your mother
_____ them? Their voices, so full of _____, taste as sweet as the
your sharpest sense   _type of love you lacked in_
                                                    childhood
juiciest _____ .
     your favorite fruit to slice
     for an after-school snack

Listen: the sea continues to _____ despite your heart's apocalyptic shattering.
                         verb of motion
_____ is waiting on the other end of the phone to remind you of
your best friend's name

_____ until you remember how to believe it.
the source of the light in
your eyes

Another _____ passes. You learn to _____ again.
     unit of time or emotion   _hope_

SYNOPHRYS

Little rebels, ungoverned by wax or by thread,
no longer subject to the disapproval
of gossiping aunties—rejoice
and multiply! It's springtime and you are in bloom
below the arch of my brow, twisted permanently
into an anxious furrow.

My friends, my friends, I name each of you
after the loved ones whose faces pixelate
across my phone screen. How cruel was I
to once have armed myself with tweezers
and plucked you, dear ones, from the root.
But fear no more! Arise and take your rightful place
as my quarantine companions, joined by your comrades
sprouting freely above my lip.

Someday, perhaps I will return
to the vinyl seat slicked with thigh sweat
where the eyebrow lady's strong hands
pull my skin taut as she threads the hairs
into submission (another small intimacy
I have taken for granted), but for now
you are my unruly allies
in this strange struggle with aloneness.
We grow wild together.

A VEGETARIAN GOES TO H MART

to finger the refrigerated meats. Something about forbidden
fruit, how the flesh gives beneath my fingertips,
makes me lick my lips with pleasure. My gorge rises
as I imagine tearing into the muscle and sinew
of raw pork belly, sucking the juice off the bone, bursting
with carnality. I grit my teeth through the revulsion
because one can never truly shed animal instinct.
In the seafood aisle, my lungs fill with the stench
of fish, a potpourri of fresh death. I don't turn away
from the milky eyes and viscous tentacles
of a neatly-packaged octopus because my people
aren't afraid to look death in the face. We eat our fish
with the heads still on and pick the bones out of our teeth
at the dinner table. Some call it impolite, but I call it
lack of pretense. A thousand vacant eyes
stare back at me, open-mouthed, as if to say
someday, you too will be gutted.
Until then, I feast.

PART THREE

LET THE MOON WOBBLE

OWED TO MY FATHER'S ACCENT

The way the letter "r" rumbles
from the cavern of his throat
through the top of his teeth, gently,
a passing freight train or a faraway
thunderstorm. The alchemy
of his language: *eavesdropped*
becomes *ear dropped* and *flirting*
becomes *floating*. The way he says
my mother's name, soft "th" sculpted solid,
syllables ringing clear like notes
from a gamelan. The way I train my tongue
to imitate his, words clumsy and labored
in my impostor mouth. The way the plumber
shakes my father's hand and says, *I'll call you
Bill instead*. The way my teachers
refuse his gaze as they ask me
to translate his English into my own.
The way he used to rub my back
on sleepless nights, his hands cracked
into tectonic plates. The same hands
that sold churros from a cart on the boardwalk.
Scrubbed grime out of a movie star's
kitchen sink. Loaded boxes of frozen food
into an eighteen-wheeler truck by moonlight.
The same hands that never learned how to use
chopsticks. The way he has to ask for a fork
when we go to our favorite noodle house.
The way the waiter says, *How spicy
do you want your food*? and my father replies,
Make me cry. The way my father does not speak
while he eats, bent over the bowl
in reverence. The way he taught me
that long noodles signify
a long life, and to cut them

is bad luck. So we slurp them up
so loudly, the whole room
stops to look.

YEAR OF THE PIG

With a round and fat face, the Pig is the symbol of wealth,
felicity, honesty, and practicality in Chinese zodiac culture.
—chinahighlights.com

My mother, my father, and I were all born in the year of the pig. The three little pigs, my mother called us.

Quietly, I resented our shared pigness. Anything would have been better than that ugly, snout-nosed creature, all dirt and gluttony.

To be as ferocious as a tiger, as clever as a monkey, as lovable as a dog—

Does every animal long to be a different kind of beast?

Does a snake lie tossing and turning in its snake-bed, dreaming itself a fearsome dragon, awakening with flame still white-hot on its tongue?

I have been known to talk with my mouth full, to leave cracker crumbs in the bedsheets, to abandon my dishes soaking in the sink for days at a time, to let my produce grow fuzzy and forgotten in the drawer.

The main difference between a pig and a hog is their level of domestication.

In a dream, I roll around in the mud, snorting and squealing in delight.

Despite my skin, despite my manners, despite the dust bunnies holding assembly beneath my bed—

More than anything, I want to make my people proud.

When I say *my people*, I mean those who have held my hand through heartbreak and bad acid trips, those whose names have been forgotten or erased, those whose blood I do and do not share.

My father[1] *is an immigrant*, I say to my grandmother[2] at the dinner table after she has tired out another tirade about immigrants ruining the country. I'm fourteen years old, teeth newly unmetaled. My cousins' jaws halt mid-chew.

Silence deadens the air around me.

Wild hogs are only known to attack humans in rare circumstances, when they feel cornered or threatened.

They will lunge towards their assailant, tearing through tissue and tendon.

That's different, my grandmother tells me, flustered. *I mean the ones who sneak in over the border.*

Feral swine are called by many names, writes the US Department of Agriculture. No matter the name, *they are a dangerous, destructive, invasive species.*

I am only as dangerous as the world demands me to be. Inside my closed mouth, my canines sharpen.

To protect native wildlife, hunters in Texas are given unrestricted license to kill hogs freely, able to shoot as many as they wish or capture and sell them as exotic meat.

The goal is not eradication, but control.

In a photograph, I hold my father's hand outside the courtroom at his citizenship ceremony.

We each wave a tiny American flag and wear a dazzling American grin.

---

[1] brown
[2] white

NOT GAY AS IN HAPPY—

Queer as in death to cops and politicians!
May they live their every waking moment
afraid of what the people will do to them.
Not queer like a rainbow slapped
onto a Wells Fargo debit card, gay as in
let's hurl a Molotov cocktail thru the window
of the bank at nightfall and kiss while we watch
the glass shatter like a supernova. Not gay
as in pride flags, queer as in flagging,
as in leatherdykes and deviance, as in the way
my fist fits perfectly inside my lover,
the way their name in my notifications
makes my clit quiver, the way their mouth
makes me melt as sticky as ice cream during
a heat wave. Queer like I'm so fruity, I may as well
be a smoothie. I'm as flamboyant as a flamingo
and as buoyant as a bumblebee blowing
bubbles behind a bounce house. Gay like
the ex-girlfriend of my ex-girlfriend is my
ex-girlfriend and we're all going dancing
in matching pleather pants. This pride month,
I'm partnering with the freaks and the fairies
to strike fear into the hearts of fascists. Let's
untether our shame and toss it in the dumpster,
let's shout this prayer so loud our lungs
collapse: Dear God, dear Björk, dear
Everything, may the fruits inherit the earth.
May the future we deserve spring into being
with a swish of our limp wrists.

FRUIT ÉTUDES

BLACKBERRY
Invasive species according
to whom? Inconsiderate, perhaps,
choking out your neighbors
by slurping up all the light. Still,
when I spot you glistening
and fat on the vine, I want
to weep sticky tears of joy
while I toss you into my mouth.

TOMATO
Like you, I've been mistaken
for a vegetable. When you're
as dependable, hearty, and thick
as we are, people forget you're
still just a tender little fruit.

RAMBUTAN
Hairy alien testicle on the outside,
slimy alien egg on the inside. You
delicious freak of nature, I'd scour
every bustling market in every
last Chinatown on earth just to find you.

DURIAN
How I long to be more like you—
audacious in your stink, your funk,
despite the disgust that bubbles up
in every room you enter. Anyone
who has never braved your jagged
armor, your brazen stench,
to devour the creamy meat beneath
doesn't know what they're missing.

MANGO

The world doesn't need more
mango diaspora poetry, proclaims
a viral tweet. I hit the block button.
Dear mango, my sweetest childhood
friend, my most sinless indulgence,
you deserve every poem you get,
including this one.

WEWE GOMBEL SPEAKS

They demanded blood, so here
      I am, ready to sink my jagged teeth
into anyone foolish enough to threaten
      what is mine. I used to think
that if I mothered each mouth that offered
      itself to me, then my womb would follow.
Instead, I am reduced to this
      cautionary tale: *Beware the barren*
woman. A bedtime whisper to frighten
      children into sleep and mothers
into compliance, while the sharp
      howls of their loneliness
knife their way into my wilted spine.
      Yes, I loved each child as though
they were my own, tucked them behind
      my papaya breasts where no cruelty
could touch, combed their matted hair
      and suckled them to honeyed
sleep. Like you, I know what it's like to want
      so badly to be loved
that you would follow any voice that called
      your name, would surrender self
for just a moment of recognition. I see
      you. I am not afraid.

PASSION FRUIT

Gorgeous moon, bright-eyed and listless.
Gorgeous slimy fruit, sour and sweet. Gorgeous
lips, hips, dimples dappling
your lower back. Gorgeous fingers vanish
into gorgeous wet. Gorgeous oblivion,
obliterating, oblivious to everything
but open. Your craving cavern
of need, delicious and depraved. Gorgeous
demand, denial, deference. Then,
gorgeous yes. Gorgeous,
yes. Darling. How gorgeously
each word from your gorgeous mouth
becomes a gorgeous, fleeting god.

THE LOVE MUSEUM IS OFFERING FREE ADMISSION

plus a 20% discount at the gift shop for anyone
on the precipice of heartbreak. I've been
meaning to go for over a year, but I was too busy
holding hands and staring into my lover's

butthole and other things that people do
when they're in love. Today, I lint roll
the cat hair off my flannel and take endless
selfies at the museum's marble steps, until

I get one where the light hits my teeth
just right and each nostril hair is in
its proper place. The main exhibit demonstrates
the history of kissing using state-of-the-art

androids with anatomically correct tongues
that undulate like mating slugs. I glide
through hallways lined with artifacts—the purple
plastic vibrator my first love gave me

for Christmas, *The L Word* DVD box set
I watched religiously in secret—and peruse
the archives of late-night texts from lovers
whose birthmarks I've willed myself to forget.

In the gift shop, I buy a souvenir: an exact replica
of the moon from the day we met, as round and shiny
as a fish egg. While I wait for the bus, I release
the moon from its box and watch it float away,

blooming like a flour tortilla in the cast-iron sky.

KISSING THE ROSE

O dirty secret, puckered aperture,
little well I have whispered my wishes
into, you greet me clenched like a jawbone
on a sleepless night. Quotidian embarrassment,
asterisk to a forbidden paragraph,
I lizard-tongue into your eager heat,
tease the thin membrane between pleasure
and disgust. O beads of sweat bedazzling
your skin, I lap you up until you're soaked
in salt and brine. Outside, the envious night
dulls its gleaming teeth. I heave my thighs
over your greedy mouth and take my turn.

ON BEING ASKED, *WHAT IS YOUR DREAM JOB?*

The cops fall dead at my feet, daisies blooming
from their gaping mouths, so I make bouquets
for all my friends and pluck petals to place
behind their ears. Our cheeks hurt from smiling

as the cages collapse into piles of dust.
My palm fits into theirs, and no venom
drips from a stranger's mouth when we dillydally
down the street. The grass grows tall and wild

beneath our soles, watered by the blood
of billionaires. Our skin is set aglow
by the Capitol sparking into flames,
painting the sky a brilliant tangerine.

Of course I do not waste my precious dreams
on labor.

CHERRY BLOSSOMS

After the most recent mass shooting, I leave my apartment for the first time in six days to buy myself flowers at Trader Joe's.

In my absence, the cherry blossoms have already begun spilling their cotton candy guts onto the sidewalk.

I've learned the shooter's face against my will. It is white and unremarkable.

Last spring I missed the blooms entirely, too fearful of the virus to risk a nonessential walk to the park less than a mile away.

By now, my fear has calcified into a pebble rattling around in my boot, rubbing my soles raw.

On my way to the store, I scroll past photos of the victims, avoiding their eyes. The dread of recognition tightening my throat.

He is everywhere: standing in line to buy coffee, watching his dog piss on a daffodil, behind me in the frozen food aisle. I capture him in my periphery.

I take inventory of my body, which parts are weapon and which are liability. My keys stay vigilant between my knuckles.

Bouquets of out-of-season sunflowers rest in metal buckets by the automatic doors, their stems drooping beneath the weight of their stubborn yellow heads.

I purchase as many as I can carry, clutching them to my chest.

At the crosswalk, a man stares at me until I shrink. His hatred and desire sharpen to a single deadly point.

He flashes an acidic grin and the cherry blossoms shiver.

Soon, the branches will be undressed once again, their soft pink garments crushed beneath a sea of careless feet.

POEM BEGINNING WITH YOU AND ENDING WITH EVERYTHING

You give me the last raspberry
from your garden, a tiny burst
of sweetness that fits on the pad
of my pinky finger. You offer me
the softest parts of your body to sink
my teeth into when I'm overcome
with wanting. You call my pharmacy
and get my meds refilled when I'm too
despondent to dial the phone.
I come over and wash the stack
of cups and bowls that have
accumulated into a small mountain
on your bedside table. I give you
my blood in a heart-shaped vial
to wear around your neck. You study
how I make my coffee, how I like
to be touched, curtail your urge
to devour, unthinking, and learn
instead to coax pleasure from my
strange and particular body. We no
longer speak, but when I fall ill,
I still make tea the way you taught me:
ginger and honey with a clove of garlic
and a dash of hot sauce to clear
the sinuses. We no longer speak,
but I'm made up of a million
gestures, touches, turns of phrase
that I learned from you, every you
I've ever loved, whose sweaters
I've wept and wiped my nose on,
whose art I've hung on my walls
and letters I keep in a box beneath
my altar, whose loved shaped me
into myself. I still don't know how

to let love lay me bare beneath
its probing gaze without apologizing
for my body's failures: when I bleed
through my pants and underwear
and stain the couch with a puddle
of blood as dark as rain-soaked
asphalt, you scrub the cushions clean
before I can say a word, knowing
I'd never ask. When I'm so
constipated I can barely move
without groaning out my agonies
like a creaky, rust-coated pipe,
you make me soup with sweet potato
and lentils to soften my stools. *So this
is it*, I marvel every time I am undone
by another disgusting display
of devotion. This is what love asks
of me: to accept every gesture of care
no matter how humiliating it feels,
to let myself be witnessed in all
my unkempt, abject, leaky, embarrassing
glory. I try to be precise and contained,
to fit myself into brief, neat stanzas,
but love makes me unwieldy, long-
winded. Love writes lines that spill
over the page. Love doesn't care
about show-don't-tell or the flimsiness
of adverbs; it wants me to tell anyone
who will listen how dazzlingly,
frustratingly, terrifyingly, mundanely,
devastatingly, blessedly, earth-shatteringly,
ass-shakingly, world-makingly it fills
me. I used to think I needed
to sand my prickly edges smooth,
to temper my too-muchness and restrain
my terrible need, but every day, love
takes my face in its hands and asks,

Who are you without performance?
while I stare back as blank
as a Word doc the night before
a deadline. I wish I could cast off
this straitjacket of my own making.
I wish I could say what I mean
without cloaking myself in metaphor.
I wish I could stand before you
and let my body be nothing
but a body, no pretense
or artifice, a night sky
unblemished by stars. Love,
by which I mean God, by which
I mean the universe, by which I mean
you, let me be as unabashed
as the single long, coarse hair
curling up from your toe knuckle.
Let me revel in the excess, ecstasy,
echo, expanse, romance, fervor,
horror, pleasure, prayer, play,
swell, spill, shine, divine, thrill,
heat, wet, want, mess, miraculous,
nameless, vivid, agonizing everything.

LATE SUMMER GHAZAL

Heat so thick, I swim in my sweat. I pluck plump blackberries off the bush and suck juice from my fingers til the sunlight dwindles, my body drenched in luminous green.

Childhood summers spent squishing our toes into hot patches of asphalt, our bikes taking flight as we raced down the block, blades of grass dyeing our kneecaps green.

The temperature crawls up like ants on a carcass. Mosquitoes grow fat off my nectarine blood. I bury my limbs in the grass and let the earth reclaim me, a casket of green.

Smoke seeps in through the windows. Our faces covered, lungs aching for air. The bloodsun blazes its weary warning. A forest burns. Memory is the brightest shade of green.

Another record shattered. Another pipeline on sacred land. Another body fed to the apparatus of empire. Each one a question I cannot ignore: Ally, what will you do in the absence of green?

YOU DESERVE THE WORLD

During this latest shiny new catastrophe,
while I lie in bed and luxuriate in the silk
of my sadness, a friend's text lights up
my screen: *You deserve the world*. Not

this world, hostile and unkind, but the one
we are building in the lines of poems,
in our wildest melatonin dreams, in the dirt
of our gardens and the recipes passed down to us

in a language that we have not yet forgotten.
I catch glimpses of it in the tsunami
of voices that floods the streets after another life
is snatched from a mother's grasp, their demands

for justice impossible to ignore. I feel it
in my friend's deliberate knuckles massaging
coconut oil into my scalp, how their steady
hands unworry my brow. Everywhere I look,

aliveness. I open my cupboard to discover
the plump red face of a tomato that I forgot
to turn into pasta sauce, now blooming
soft tufts of mold, the stubborn insistence

of life in even the harshest conditions. I slice
the tip of my finger while chopping cloves of garlic,
and before the first drop of blood has blushed
the counter, it coagulates at the edge of the wound—

a miracle, this body, how it has already begun
to heal before I've even registered
the hurt. When I say, *You deserve the world*,
what I mean is this is not the first apocalypse

we have survived. The world has ended before,
and before and before, and for some, there was
no after. We have watched its rind cracking open
like a freshly-broken heart, and each time

we build and rebuild. We kiss our houseplants
on their leafy foreheads before we go
to sleep. We dress our bodies in the most
brilliant light. We dance like the empire is dying,

water the ground where it once stood, and watch
what blooms, lush and verdant, in its wake.

HYDRA

ugly as the day I was born   I carry my past like an apology
scraping dead selves   off the soles of my feet
onto the pavement   onto the organic produce at Whole Foods
onto my lover's best pillowcases   a sorry sight

elsewhere   a perfect specimen
soft-spoken   unstained underwear   graceful even in death
my god   I would kiss her
if only I could get close enough

I could have drunk   from her forever   and still thirsted
for more   yes   I know that greed
is unbecoming   but I have all these mouths
to feed   and more   with every passing minute

each self I shed   shudders with pleasure
at the rupture   each tiny death
a new freedom   still   I am embarrassed
by all this mess   I've made

out of the carnage   another head sprouts
bloody and screaming   but so wholly mine
who'd have believed   that I could birth all this bounty?

arms full of daughter   mother   wife
neck aching   from the weight   of myselves
       I rise
leaving a trail of me   in my wake

LET THE MOON WOBBLE

NOTES

"Kuburan Cina Bintaro" is titled after the name of the cemetery in Lombok, Indonesia where my grandfather is buried.

"*Self-Portrait with Cropped Hair*" is an ekphrasis on a painting with the same title by Frida Khalo.

"June 23, 1982" was written about and in memory of Vincent Chin, a Chinese-American man who was beaten to death by two white men on the titular date. The men who murdered him pled guilty to manslaughter and were sentenced to pay $3,000 and serve three years of probation, with no jail time.

"I Call Grief by My Mother's Name" takes its form from Ocean Vuong's poem "Seventh Circle of Earth."

"Heartbreak Mad Libs" takes its form from Angbeen Saleem's poem "poem mad lib for the apocalypse," and, of course, from the game Mad Libs.

"Fruit Études" is inspired by a poem of the same name by Marilyn Chin.

"Wewe Gombel Speaks" was inspired by Dena Igusti's poem "self portrait as kuntilanak." In Javanese folklore, Wewe Gombel is the ghost of a woman whose husband stopped loving her due to her infertility. When she discovered him having an affair, she killed him and then herself in a fit of despair. Now, she kidnaps neglected children, hiding them behind her long, hanging breasts and caring for them until their parents repent.

ACKNOWLEDGMENTS

Poems from this collection have appeared, sometimes in different forms, in *Queer Nature: A Poetry Anthology, Bellingham Review, The Journal, ALOCASIA, Palette Poetry, Columbia Journal,* the *2022 Jack Straw Writers Program Anthology, Muzzle Magazine, Foglifter, UNDERBLONG, UW Magazine,* the *lickety~split, Five South, Touchstone, The Shallow Ends, Shō Poetry Journal, Duende, KUOW Public Radio, Parentheses Journal, beestung, The Rumpus, We the Gathered Heat: Asian American and Pacific Islander Poetry, Performance, and Spoken Word,* and *Tahoma Literary Review.*

Boundless thanks to the editors and staff at Alice James Books for your time, attention, and care.

Thank you to the National Endowment for the Arts, Tin House, Artist Trust, the Jack Straw Cultural Center, and MacDowell for nurturing my work through the generous gift of time and resources.

To my teachers, editors, and mentors Sumita Chakraborty, Pimone Triplett, Linda Bierds, Yanyi, Faylita Hicks, Jane Wong, George Abraham, Shira Erlichman, Sarena Brown, Michael Schmeltzer, and Lisa Gluskin Stonestreet: thank you for expanding my poetics, deepening my thinking, offering support, and helping to make this book what it is.

To my blood and chosen family whose love has brought me here: Zury, Angel, Bhupi, Justice, Cass, Cody, Nic, Aathira, Forest, Jake, Anju, Bri, Josh, Nicholas, Levi, Bim, Jamie, and finally/especially to my parents, Kathleen and Wim Ang. The love I have for each of you could make the moon wobble with its gravity. Thank you for supporting me, my writing life, and the making of this book.

To my cat Gomez: since you can't read, I will give you an extra can of wet food as thanks for being my muse.

My deepest gratitude to the Duwamish and Coast Salish peoples, the Western Nehântick and Mohegan peoples, and the Pawtucket and Massachusett peoples, upon whose land these poems were written. May we all live to see liberation, from Turtle Island to Palestine and beyond.

To anyone I may have thoughtlessly omitted: Holes are my favorite things. An absence is another form of hole. So if you find yourself absent from these pages know you are my hole, a favorite.

RECENT TITLES FROM ALICE JAMES BOOKS

The Seeds, Cecily Parks
All the Possible Bodies, Iain Haley Pollock
Saint Consequence, Michael M. Weinstein
Freeland, Leigh Sugar
Mothersalt, Mia Ayumi Malhotra
When the Horses, Mary Helen Callier
Cold Thief Place, Esther Lin
If Nothing, Matthew Nienow
Zombie Vomit Mad Libs, Duy Đoàn
The Holy & Broken Bliss, Alicia Ostriker
Wish Ave, Alessandra Lynch
Autobiomythography of, Ayokunle Falomo
Old Stranger: Poems, Joan Larkin
I Don't Want To Be Understood, Joshua Jennifer Espinoza
Canandaigua, Donald Revell
In the Days That Followed, Kevin Goodan
Light Me Down: The New & Collected Poems of Jean Valentine, Jean Valentine
Song of My Softening, Omotara James
Theophanies, Sarah Ghazal Ali
Orders of Service, Willie Lee Kinard III
The Dead Peasant's Handbook, Brian Turner
The Goodbye World Poem, Brian Turner
The Wild Delight of Wild Things, Brian Turner
I Am the Most Dangerous Thing, Candace Williams
Burning Like Her Own Planet, Vandana Khanna
Standing in the Forest of Being Alive, Katie Farris
Feast, Ina Cariño
Decade of the Brain: Poems, Janine Joseph
American Treasure, Jill McDonough
We Borrowed Gentleness, J. Estanislao Lopez
Brother Sleep, Aldo Amparán
Sugar Work, Katie Marya
Museum of Objects Burned by the Souls in Purgatory, Jeffrey Thomson
Constellation Route, Matthew Olzmann

Alice James Books is committed to publishing books that matter. The press was founded in 1973 in Boston, Massachusetts to give women access to publishing. As a cooperative, authors performed the day-to-day undertakings of the press. The press continues to expand and grow from its formative roots, guided by its founding values of access, excellence, inclusivity, and collaboration in publishing. Its mission is to publish books that matter and preserve a place of belonging for poets who inspire us. AJB seeks to broaden our collective interpretation of what constitutes the American poetic voice and is dedicated to helping its artists achieve purposeful engagement with broad audiences and communities nationwide. The press was named for Alice James, sister to William and Henry, whose extraordinary gift for writing went unrecognized during her lifetime.

Designed by Tiani Kennedy

Printed by Versa Press